Extreme Science Jobs

John DiConsiglio

SCHOLASTIC INC.

New York   Toronto   London   Auckland   Sydney
Mexico City   New Delhi   Hong Kong   Buenos Aires

Cover
© Therese Frare/www.evergreen.edu/ican

Developed by ONO Books in cooperation with Scholastic Inc.

ISBN 0-439-59805-2

1 2 3 4 5 6 7 8 9 10   08   12 11 10 09 08 07 06 05 04 03

Contents

Welcome to This Book

Do you like adventure? Well, get ready. It's time for some extreme science!

Science can take you to the bottom of the ocean. It can lead you up the trunk of a giant tree, or into the mouth of a volcano. You can hunt for the world's deadliest diseases—then go to the heart of the jungle looking for their cures.

The scientists you're about to meet risk their lives to track down clues to scientific mysteries. So hang on. You're coming along for the ride!

Target Words

Here are some words that will help you understand these science adventures.

- **awe:** fear and wonder

  With awe, the scientist watched the volcano erupt.

- **descend:** to go lower down

  Evan will descend to the bottom of the sea to learn about the creatures that live there.

- **predict:** to try to guess the future

  If scientists learn to predict when a volcano will erupt, they will save many lives.

Reader Tips

Here's how to get the most from this book.

- **Subheads** A subhead is like a title for a section of a chapter. It tells the main idea of that section. Look at the subhead, "Hot Spots," on page 7. What will this section be about?

- **Fact/Opinion** As you read, try to separate the facts from the opinions. A fact can be proven. An opinion is a feeling or belief.

1

The Volcano Climber

**Rosaly Lopes-Gautier can take the heat.
Even when it's coming from a volcano.**

Rosaly Lopes-Gautier has climbed volcanoes for 25 years. So she knows how dangerous they can be. But that doesn't stop her.

Once, Rosaly was climbing Mount Etna, a 10,000-foot mountain of rock and **lava** in Italy. She stood just a hundred feet from an **erupting** crater. She wore a gas mask and a hard hat for safety. Rosaly couldn't take her eyes off the fountains of red lava that sprayed into the sky.

But then something crashed at her feet. It was a "lava bomb." These balls of melted rock are blasted into the sky before falling to the earth. The lava bomb snapped Rosaly back to reality. And one word echoed in her brain: Run!

Hot Spots

Rosaly is a volcanologist, a scientist who studies volcanoes. She works with **NASA,** the U.S. space agency. For her job, Rosaly travels to some of the world's hottest spots. How hot? She's climbed volcanoes where the lava reaches 1,500 degrees Fahrenheit. And each time, she learns more about these strange and deadly mountains.

Most mountains sit on top of solid rock. But volcanoes are different. They form over pools of molten, or melted, rock. The melted rock simmers just below the earth's surface. When underground gas and melted rock boil up, watch out! That's when most people run for their lives.

There are about 600 active volcanoes in the world. Any of them could erupt at any time. Some are cone-shaped with a hollow center. Others look like craters in flat ground. But whatever their form, volcanoes are like outdoor labs to Rosaly.

Rosaly studies lava samples and how volcanoes form. She looks at the effects of volcanic eruptions on our weather. At NASA, Rosaly searches for signs of volcanoes on other planets.

Volcanoes also offer a look at what's inside the earth. Scientists hope to be able to **predict** when volcanoes will erupt. That could save the lives of people who live in a volcano's shadow.

Set on Science

Volcanology is an unusual career for anyone. But being a scientist of any kind was considered strange when Rosaly was a girl growing up in Brazil. There were few opportunities in that country for girls who liked science. So her mother made her take typing classes so she could become a secretary.

But Rosaly's father pushed her to follow her passion for science. "He wanted me to be an astronomer so I could name a comet after him," Rosaly jokes.

Rosaly's parents sent her to school in England to study science. It was there that she fell in love with volcanoes.

Heads Up!

Why did Rosaly take typing classes?

Rosaly stood on top of a lava flow in Hawaii.

Rosaly has studied volcanoes for years, but an eruption still fills her with **awe.** The ground trembles under her. The ear-splitting "BOOM!" signals that an explosion is near. And then…a cloud of black ash covers the sky.

"Then it's a mighty force of nature like nothing you have ever seen," Rosaly says. "There are rivers of red lava. And flying balls of fire. It's the most beautiful of nature's **spectacles.**"

That's what happened on Mount Etna. Still, Rosaly hiked to the lip of the volcano. Her boots crunched on crusted lava. It sounded like she was walking on broken glass. Rosaly looked into the volcano's cone and saw a bottomless lake of fire. Then she heard that boom.

"Some eruptions you know are coming days or weeks or months in advance," she says. "This one caught us by surprise."

Flowing lava is slow. It's easy to move out of its path. But the lava bombs are more dangerous. They exploded around Rosaly. They rained drops of ash. She ran for her life. She raced down a mountain path. She dove into her car and hit the gas. Through her rearview mirror, she saw Mount

Etna overflow with glowing red and orange lava.

It wasn't Rosaly's first close call. And it won't keep her away from volcanoes in the future. She says volcanoes offer a dazzling adventure for an experienced climber.

And if you have to make a quick getaway? "Park your car facing away from the volcano," she says. "I always keep my keys in the ignition and the motor running."

Heads Up!

Rosaly calls volcanic eruptions "the most beautiful of nature's spectacles." Is that a fact or an opinion?

Why Do Volcanoes Erupt?

Volcanoes have fascinated and frightened people for centuries. In 1980, Mount St. Helens erupted in Washington. It killed 51 people. A volcano in Italy called Vesuvius blew in 79 AD. It wiped out the entire city of Pompeii.

What causes these fiery shows? Volcanoes are open vents in the earth's surface. The vents lead deep underground.

The earth is hot inside. It's so hot that some rocks melt. They become a thick liquid called **magma.** Magma is lighter than the solid rock around it, so it rises. As it nears the surface, bubbles form.

The gas bubbles create a lot of pressure. The pressure builds until a violent eruption rips open the earth. Then the pressure can escape. Magma that reaches the surface is called lava.

The explosions can be deadly to people. But they may serve an important purpose. Scientists think volcanoes are the earth's way of releasing underground heat. Talk about blowing off steam!

SODA

The orange magma becomes lava when it reaches the surface.

2

Under the Sea

Evan B. Forde has a deep love of the water. It's really deep. He explores the ocean floor.

Thunk! That's the sound of the hatch slamming shut on Evan B. Forde's submarine. Evan has heard that dull thud at least a dozen times in his career. But it always fills his stomach with butterflies. There's no going back now, he thinks. The next stop is the ocean floor.

Evan is an oceanographer. He studies the oceans. Evan specializes in a part of the ocean that few people ever see. He explores the dark mysteries of the ocean floor.

"There are different kinds of oceanographers. Some stay close to the surface. And some, like me, go way down," Evan says.

How far down? Evan's submarine can **descend** two miles below the surface. At that depth, Evan is surrounded by pitch-black darkness. His sub cruises through underwater canyons the size of cities. And if his sub were to get stuck? No rescue ships or divers could reach him in time.

That fact bothers Evan. But still, he's not afraid to get his feet wet. He works for the National Oceanic and Atmospheric Administration. He's the first African-American scientist to do this type of research.

Evan wasn't the first person in his family who was interested in science. His father was a high school science teacher. So Evan grew up with microscopes and chemistry sets in every corner of the house. At night, he'd balance his telescope on the hood of his parents' car. From there, he'd gaze at stars.

"I wanted to be an astronaut. Or a football player," Evan says. "The last place I thought I'd end up was at the bottom of the ocean."

But Evan has spent a great deal of time there. He studies everything in the sea. He researches ocean **currents,** sea creatures, and underwater rocks and mountains. What he learns about the ocean can help us protect it from pollution.

Evan's work also helps unlock the secrets of the earth's **climate.** The oceans hold much of the earth's heat. As water slowly circulates, it moves huge amounts of heat around the planet. Those heat changes trigger harsh weather, like storms and hurricanes. Studying changes in the ocean can help us tell when extreme weather will arrive.

ALVIN

Evan does much of his work in a navy sub called an ALVIN. Just 23 feet long, it's Evan's ride to a different world.

"It's beautiful down there," Evan says. "It's dark and strange and, yeah, a little scary. You never know what you're going to see."

As it sinks to the bottom of the ocean, the inside of the ALVIN is dark. Only an instrument panel lights the gray metal walls.

Heads Up!

Oceanography is the study of everything in the ocean. Why is it important to study the oceans?

Here, Evan is inside the Deep Submergence Research Vessel
Johnson Sea Link.

The submarine is hot and stuffy. But Evan wears a warm jacket and a cap. As the ALVIN goes down, the deep water will cool the sub to near freezing.

Hundreds of feet down, the water is dark. The ALVIN has powerful headlights. But Evan can only see 15 feet ahead of him. Outside the ALVIN, strange creatures come and go out of the range of light. Evan notes giant shrimp, spider crabs, and long flat eels that glow in the dark. He spots fish with eyes that don't see. They don't need to see down there in the darkness.

Buried Two Miles Under

Each trip to the ocean floor is an adventure. But one sticks out in Evan's mind. Nearly 20 years ago, he and a pilot took the ALVIN two miles down. Evan saw an interesting rock on a canyon wall. They moved in for a closer look.

The pilot made the sub's robot arm reach out. It tugged at the rock. Suddenly, the wall crumbled. Dirt and rocks tumbled down, trapping the sub.

The propellers spun in the dirt like a car wheel stuck in the mud. But the sub wouldn't move. The pilot gunned the engine. Evan sweated. He wondered if the ALVIN would become their deep-sea coffin. No rescuers could reach them there.

After ten long, scary minutes, the sub broke free. The pilot slapped Evan on the back. "Okay," he laughed nervously. "You can breathe now."

"Down there, you want to have a strong stomach and steady sea legs," Evan says. "And, oh yeah, a little bit of luck can't hurt."

It was a frightening event. But Evan has repeated the plunge many times since then. He loves the thrill of diving into a barely known part of the planet. And he loves the thrill of coming back up, too.

Heads Up!

Describe what it's like in the submarine two miles underwater.

3

Nalini of the Rain Forest

Like a modern-day Tarzan, Nalini Nadkarni scrambles up rain forest trees.

It's dark and quiet on the floor of the Costa Rican rain forest. Huge trees block most of the sunlight. On the ground, the forest looks almost lifeless.

But Nalini Nadkarni has left the ground far behind. She's climbing a 200-foot-high tree called a strangler fig. Gripping a climbing rope, she pulls herself over the branches. Above, she can see the blue of the Central American sky.

Suddenly, her head pops through the treetops. It's sunny, loud, and bursting with life. She's surrounded by a green sea of leaves high above the forest shadows. Brightly colored birds and insects whirl in the **canopy** around her.

"It's a stirring, beautiful, awesome experience," Nalini says. "It's like entering another **realm.**"

Until a few years ago, no one had ever been here. Well, no one but monkeys, bugs, and birds. Nalini helped change that.

She's an ecologist. That's a scientist who studies living things and their environments. She works at Evergreen State College in Washington. But her research often takes her to the rain forest. There, she puts her mountain-climbing skills to good use. She became one of the first people to scale these sky-scraping trees.

At the top, Nalini does more than just enjoy the view. She takes pictures and collects samples. And she has discovered new **species** of plants and animals. Nalini's research tells us about the rain forest's **ecosystem.** An ecosystem is a community of living things and their environment. Nalini has found plants that have helped scientists develop

Heads Up!

Look up realm *in the glossary. What does Nalini mean when she says being in the rain forest is like entering another realm?*

new medicines. And she hopes her work will help people realize how valuable the rain forest is.

Crazy About Climbing

Nalini has never been a stranger to treetops. As a child, maples and elms lined the driveway of her Maryland home. She'd hurry home from school, grab a snack, and say a quick hello to her mom. Then she'd pick up a book and head for the trees. There, she'd balance herself on the highest branch. "It always felt like my own little world," she says.

In school, Nalini studied dance. But the outdoors seemed more exciting than the stage. As an ecologist, she's hiked the woods of the Pacific Northwest. She's explored tropical forests. But tree canopies presented the tallest challenge.

Scientists had guessed that as many as 30 million species of plants and animals lived in the

Heads Up!

Nalini wants people to realize how valuable the rain forest is. What are some ways that the rain forest is valuable?

22

treetops. But nobody knew for sure. They couldn't get there to start counting.

Then Nalini had a simple idea. Why not climb the trees? A rain forest tree can be as high as a 25-story building. Each branch holds stinging insects and poisonous thorns. Some scientists laughed at Nalini's idea. They called it "Tarzan and Jane stuff," she recalls.

Nalini was determined. She traveled to Costa Rica with her own invention. It was a new kind of crossbow. From the ground, Nalini aimed it into the branches. She shot an arrow into the air. It carried a thin rope over a branch 125 feet up. That's about half the way to the top of the tallest tree. Then, she used the thin rope to pull a heavier rope over the tree limb. Then she connected it to a climbing harness.

Now Nalini could begin her long climb up the tree. "I looked like an inchworm crawling up the side of a mountain," Nalini says. Bees swarmed in her hair. Rock-hard "bullet ants" bit her legs. But nothing stopped her. Standing on a high branch, Nalini pulled in her line. She took aim and fired again.

Finally, Nalini broke through to the sunlight. She had become one of the few humans ever to reach the rain forest canopy.

The leaves seemed to move like waves. She touched plants that no one on the earth had ever seen before. Hummingbirds landed on her shoulder. A howler monkey watched her from a nearby tree. "The sights, the sounds, the smells. It overwhelms your senses," she says.

Nalini has climbed hundreds of trees since. Each one is different, she says. Years after a climb, she'll return to a rain forest. She remembers the trees like old friends.

"I know their trunks and their leaves and their branches," Nalini says. "And they give me everything from oxygen to information. Sometimes I'll be nestled in a branch, and I'll feel like the arms of the tree are holding me. It's the nicest place in the world."

Heads Up!

Getting into the rain forest canopy was difficult. How did Nalini do it?

As a child, Nalini climbed trees for fun. Now she climbs them for science.

4

The Virus Hunters

This husband-and-wife science team battles killer diseases.

The small plane touched down on a grassy airstrip in Sudan, a country in eastern Africa. Joseph McCormick and several other scientists unloaded their equipment. As soon as it was light enough, their pilot took off. His message was clear: *Good luck, docs. But I'm not sticking around. Not while a killer disease is on the loose.*

The team of doctors couldn't blame the pilot. A bumpy jeep ride later, they arrived at a hospital. The building was really just a hut. It had walls made of mud and a roof made of straw. It had no windows at all.

Holding kerosene lamps, the doctors visited dozens of patients. The lucky ones had straw mattresses. Others lay on the bare floor. Many were weak and throwing up. Most had fevers. Their foreheads were covered in sweat.

The hospital staff was puzzled. What could possibly make these people so sick?

The answer, the doctors found, was Ebola. This disease has killed thousands of people in Africa. McCormick now knew what he was up against: a killer **virus.** And he settled in to see if the virus could be fought with medicine.

Virus Hunting

Joseph McCormick is a virologist from the University of Texas. He teams up with his wife, Dr. Susan Fisher-Hoch. Together they battle viruses that cause terrible diseases. The couple treats patients and looks for cures.

The two doctors come from very different backgrounds. Susan grew up in England. At first, she had wanted to be an actress. But then she fell in love with science. Joseph grew up in Tennessee.

Heads Up!

The word part -ologist means "one who studies." What does Joseph study?

He became a volunteer teacher in Zaire. Seeing the disease and suffering there made him decide to study medicine, too.

An outbreak of a strange illness anywhere in the world puts this pair of doctors on the next plane. They've traveled from Nigeria to Saudi Arabia to China. One long-term project took them to Sierra Leone, on and off, for 15 years. There they fought a deadly disease called Lassa Fever. Lassa Fever kills thousands of people each year in West Africa.

Invisible Killers

Viruses are tiny creatures, much smaller than the eye can see. They're **parasites** that attack plants and animals. They can't live without a **host** to feed upon. The host could be a flower or a dog. Or it could be you.

When a virus gets into a person, it invades the cells. There, it can copy itself into an army of millions. The virus then spreads throughout the body, attacking healthy cells. Some viruses cause common illnesses, like the flu. Others are deadly, like HIV. That's the virus that causes AIDS.

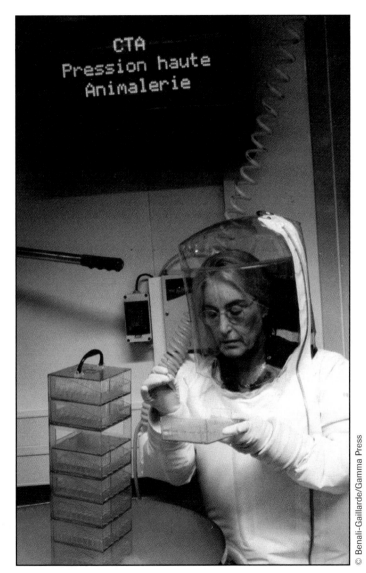

Susan had to wear a protective suit to take this deadly virus sample out of storage.

In the field, Joseph and Susan take blood samples from patients. They study and identify the virus. Then they create a plan to try to battle the disease.

Often, they do studies to try to develop **vaccines.** These medicines can keep healthy people from getting the disease. People need vaccines because viruses cannot be cured.

Joseph and Susan also teach health-care workers how to keep the virus from spreading. They show hospital workers how to throw away **infected** objects, like used needles. Sometimes they even recommend a quarantine. That's when no one in an infected area is allowed to leave. One sick person could spread a virus to another town, or even another country. And if a virus spreads too far, it can become almost unstoppable.

"We are always racing to keep one step ahead of these viruses," Susan says. "But they are usually one step ahead of us."

"Like detectives, we piece together clues to find where the viruses are hiding," Joseph adds. "If we catch them, maybe we can learn enough to wipe them out."

But sometimes their work gets interrupted. Joseph and Susan's project in Sierra Leone closed down in 1991 when the country had a bloody civil war. Still, on one of their lasts visits, they had an experience that made all the dangerous work seem worthwhile.

As their truck bounced along dirt roads, Susan saw villagers running to meet them. Joseph hit the brakes. Soon, their truck was surrounded by dozens of people. Some of them were the patients who had been so sick. They wanted to thank Joseph and Susan for saving their lives.

"Now and then, we have our victories," Joseph says. "In many of these countries, the people are poor and the hospitals are bad. When someone gets sick, the odds are against him. It's amazing to see them healthy again."

Heads Up!

Why were the villagers so thankful to Joseph and Susan?

5

The Jungle Drugstore

Eloy Rodriguez hunts for new medicines.
Wild animals show him the way.

Eloy Rodriguez works in the Impenetrable Forest of Uganda. It's called impenetrable because it's nearly impossible to walk through. To get to work, Eloy hacks through thick elephant grass. Sometimes he tiptoes around deadly black scorpions and tarantulas. If a flying beetle hits him in the head, he could be knocked out. These beetles are as hard as rocks. Eloy also avoids the poisoned spikes that stick out from some trees.

Eloy is a biologist at Cornell University. He studies plants and animals. Now he's on a jungle mission looking for cures. For what? You name it: malaria, AIDS, the common cold. He watches how animals use plants to treat their illnesses. Then he sees if those plants can also help people.

Sometimes Eloy studies how gorillas use plants. He might find some gorillas in a clearing in the jungle. Usually they are lying on rocks or leaning against trees. A gorilla leader is called a silverback male. They can weigh up to five hundred pounds. Eloy knows the gorillas are peaceful creatures, most of the time.

Eloy tries to keep his distance from the gorillas. He doesn't want to disturb them. He is watching to see what sick gorillas do. Once he saw some hobble to a bush. They picked out the prickly leaves. Then they shoved the leaves in their mouths, spines and all. A few hours later, they seemed to be feeling better.

"Just follow the animals," Eloy says. They'll lead you to the next scientific breakthrough. He calls it "zoopharmacognosy" (zoo-*far*-muh-KOG-nuh-see). "We owe every drug we have to nature," he says.

Heads Up!

Why doesn't Eloy want to disturb the animals he watches?

Rocky Road to Science

Eloy worked hard to become a scientist. He grew up in a poor Mexican-American town in Texas. His father took whatever jobs he could find, from peach picker to short-order cook. His mother cleaned teachers' houses.

"She was like a spy in a different culture," Eloy says. "She saw the books they read. And she passed them on to me."

Eloy graduated at the top of his class. Still, his counselor told him to skip college and become a car mechanic.

"I didn't know the first thing about cars," Eloy recalls.

But Eloy had bigger dreams. His large family valued education. Of his 67 cousins, 64 graduated from college. "We were poor, but we weren't stupid," he says. And the school's attitude was not very respectful.

In his work, Eloy has learned to respect the ways of animals and humans. In Venezuela, he once tagged along with an Indian tribe called the Piaroa (Pee-ah-row-ah). As they hunted, the Piaroa showed Eloy a leafy plant. They told him

Eloy has learned a lot about healing plants from watching animals.

it eased the pain of wasp stings. Now scientists are turning that leaf into an important new painkiller. In Peru, a monkey led Eloy to a flower. Now that flower may become a new cancer treatment.

Eloy usually blends right in when he does his research. But he knows when he's not wanted. He spent weeks tracking a band of gorillas in Uganda. Then one day, they decided they were tired of Eloy.

"They charged right at me," he says. "When you get thumped by a five-hundred-pound silverback, you know it's time to gather your plants and go back to the lab."

Heads Up!

How does Eloy's work help people who are sick?

Nature in Your Medicine Cabinet

What do you do when you have a headache? You probably wouldn't think of munching on a willow tree. That may sound strange, but it's not. The main ingredient in aspirin is willow bark.

Do you like garlic on your pizza? Then you may need some mouthwash. And where do you think that minty-fresh taste comes from? It comes from the oil in a minty-tasting leaf.

Drug companies spend a lot of money making medicines. What are the important ingredients in many of them? Plants. Scientists have put plants into everything from painkillers to mouthwash.

But plants can do more than get rid of headaches and make your breath smell good. Somewhere in your house, you may have a sticky syrup called Ipecac. It's made from a plant by the same name. When people accidentally swallow poison, Ipecac helps them vomit it back up. It has actually saved lives.

Who knows what other life-saving plants are out there just waiting to be found!

6

The Mummy Finder

Johan Reinhard will go anywhere to dig up secrets of the past.

She's called Juanita. But nobody knows her real name. She's been dead for more than 500 years. Juanita was a young **Inca** girl. She lived in a South American **empire** that stretched from Colombia to Chile.

Here's what experts think happened to her. One day around 1470, she was led to the top of Mount Ampato. The 20,000 foot mountain rises over southern Peru. There, she was killed by a blow to the head.

Juanita was a human **sacrifice.** It sounds horrible. But it was probably a great honor in her time. Families offered their teenage girls to the gods. It was believed that such sacrifices protected the people from disaster.

Juanita's body might have stayed on that mountain forever. That is if Johan Reinhard hadn't come along. He's one of the world's top archaeologists. He learns about ancient people by studying the things they left behind.

"Every time you find something—whether it's clothes or a statue or a Juanita—it's like looking into a window to the past," says Johan. He works as an explorer with the National Geographic Society. But mummies are his passion.

Many Kinds of Mummies

But wait, you might think. Aren't mummies those Egyptian bodies that look like they're wrapped in bandages from head to toe? Actually, a mummy is any dead body that's been **preserved** for a long time.

Juanita was preserved by the cold mountain air. Then centuries of snow and ice buried her. But Mount Ampato is near a volcano. Over time, the gray ash from the volcano melted the ice around Juanita. That's when Johan found her.

Johan has a knack for finding buried stuff. When he was a child, he dug holes in his Illinois backyard looking for arrowheads and fossils. And in his attic, he found dust-covered Hardy Boys books. Those are mysteries that star two teenage brothers. Flipping through their yellowed pages, he fell in love with mystery and adventure.

Mystery and adventure are what Johan loves about archaeology. One project took him into underwater caves in the Mediterranean Sea. That's where he uncovered ancient Roman works of art.

Johan has also lived with camel herders in the Great Indian Desert. And he's hung out with fishermen on the Maldives Islands in the Indian Ocean. Johan will search anywhere to dig up clues to the past.

Meeting Juanita

Johan wasn't looking for mummies when he climbed Mount Ampato. He was actually there to take pictures of the neighboring volcano.

Heads Up!

Johan says he loves the mystery and adventure of his job. Is that a fact or an opinion?

Johan's job has taken him to icy peaks, deserts, and even caves under the sea.

But as he got near the peak, he saw red feathers sticking out of the ground. He recognized them. They were part of an Incan headdress.

As he got closer, Johan saw a large bundle. At first, he thought it was a backpack. Then his heart began to race. That was no backpack. It was a person.

Juanita's face was frozen in what Johan called a "peaceful" expression. She was wearing a fancy chocolate-colored gown with red and white stripes. Her long black hair was frozen as if it were still waving in the mountain wind.

Johan knew the importance of his discovery. No well-preserved Incan mummies had ever been found before. But how could he get a ninety-pound dead girl down a 20,000 foot mountain? He couldn't leave her up there. She might be attacked by birds. Or she might be raided by treasure-seeking looters.

Johan wrapped Juanita in a sleeping bag. He strapped her to his back and carefully climbed down the icy mountain path. Then, he tied her to a mule and went into town. She finally made it to Johan's lab in the baggage hold of a bus.

How did Johan figure out what happened to Juanita? Near her body, he found items left as presents, or offerings, to the gods. Later, X-rays showed that Juanita's skull had been crushed. She was killed by a blow above her right eye. These clues matched old stories about Incan child sacrifices. A Spanish priest had witnessed these events in the 1600s and written about them.

Today, Juanita is a celebrity. When she's not at home at a university in Peru, she's on a world tour. Like a rock star, she's visited the United States and Japan. "In a way, I guess she will live forever," Johan says. "But we'll never know who she really was. Some of the past always remains a mystery."

Heads Up!

Johan says that, in a way, Juanita "will live forever." What does he mean by this?

Johan's assistant, Miguel Zarate, is holding Juanita.

How to Make a Mummy

Juanita's body was preserved by the cold. But the ancient Egyptians came up with a way to make mummies themselves. Here's how.

Step 1 Embalmers washed the body. They rinsed it with water from the Nile river.

Step 2 They removed the liver, lungs, stomach, and intestines. They dried them in salt and stored them in jars, which were later buried with the mummy.

Step 3 Egyptians believed that the heart was the center of intelligence and feeling. So they cut it out, dried it, and returned it to the body.

Step 4 They pulled out the brain through the nose. They thought it was worthless.

Step 5 They replaced the eyes with glass eyeballs.

Step 6 They stuffed the body with salt, which they left in for 40 days.

Step 7 After removing the salt, the embalmers washed the body and wrapped it with long strips of linen cloth.

Glossary

awe *(noun)* fear and wonder (p. 10)

canopy *(noun)* the top layer in a forest, formed by dense, leaf-covered branches (p. 20)

climate *(noun)* the system of a planet's weather (p.16)

current *(noun)* the movement of water in a river or ocean (p. 15)

descend *(verb)* to go lower down (p. 14)

ecosystem *(noun)* a community of living things and their environment (p. 21)

empire *(noun)* different lands belonging to one ruler (p. 38)

erupt *(verb)* to suddenly and violently explode (p. 6)

host *(noun)* a plant or animal that another organism lives in and feeds upon (p. 28)

Inca *(noun)* an Indian tribe that ruled a vast empire in South America about 500 years ago (p. 38)

infected *(adjective)* dirty or poisoned (p. 30)

lava *(noun)* the hot, liquid rock that pours out of a volcano when it erupts (p. 6)

magma *(noun)* melted rock deep underground; it becomes lava if it reaches the surface through a volcano (p. 12)

NASA *(noun)* National Aeronautics and Space Administration (p. 7)

parasite *(noun)* an animal that lives off another animal's body (p. 28)

predict *(verb)* to try to guess the future (p. 8)

preserve *(verb)* to keep from rotting (p. 39)

realm *(noun)* a kingdom or world (p. 21)

sacrifice *(noun)* the offering of something to a god (p. 38)

species *(noun)* a type of animal or plant (p. 21)

spectacle *(noun)* a display or show (p. 10)

vaccine *(noun)* a medicine that prevents a person from getting a disease (p. 30)

virus *(noun)* a tiny organism that attacks the cells of plants and animals (p. 27)

Index